The Movie Quiz & Trivia Book Vol. 1 (The Oscars)

AUTHOR

B D Petty

ISBN: 9798865308379

Acknowledgements

All material in this book has been researched by the author using the following resources, and is accurate at the time of publication, November 2023. The answers are all related to the year the films either won or were nominated for an Academy Award, not the year in which films were released.

IMDb

Filmsite.org

Oscars.org

ScreenRant

Google

Britannica.com

AARP.org

Reuters

Movieweb.com

CONTENTS

TRIVIA

The winner of the first Academy Award for Best Picture (at the time the category was *Outstanding Picture*), was the film 'WINGS' in 1929. It was the film that helped launch the career of a young Gary Cooper, who later went on to win two Best Actor Oscars: one in 1942 for the film "Sergeant York" and the other in 1953 for the film "High Noon".

BEST PICTURE WINNERS

Using the three clues provided, test your knowledge, and work out what these Best Picture winning films are...

FILM 1

1. This American legal drama was based on a 1977 novel by Avery Corman.

2. Justin Henry plays a young boy in the middle of a family custody battle.

3. Both Dustin Hoffman and Meryl Streep received Oscars for their roles in this film at the 1980 Academy Awards.

ANSWER: _____

FILM 2

1. This film won 11 of its 12 Oscar nominations at the 1960 Awards Ceremony.

2. Filmed on location in Italy, it was the most expensive film created at the point of release, costing $15 million.

3. The famous chariot race scene took three weeks to film and used 15,000 extras.

ANSWER: _____

FILM 3

1. Winner of seven Academy Awards at the 1971 ceremony, one for Writing (based on factual material) by Francis Ford Coppola and Edmund H. North.

2. Although winning the Best Actor Category, its star refused to collect his award; telegramming the Academy telling them that he wanted his name removing from the list of nominees.

3. It is an epic biographical war film about a Second World War U.S General.

ANSWER: _____

FILM 4

1. This film was the first movie sequel to win an Oscar.

2. This film not only won Best Picture Oscar, but also gave Robert De Niro his first of two Academy Awards. This one in the category of 'Best Supporting Actor'.

3. In 1991 the third film in this trilogy was nominated for 7 Oscars but did not win any.

ANSWER: _____

FILM 5

1. Nominated for 13 Academy Awards, this film won 6, including Best Actor and Best Picture at the 1995 ceremony.

2. The film is based on a novel of the same name from 1986, by Winston Groom.

3. A famous quote from this film is, 'Momma always said, Life is like a box of Chocolates. You never know what you're gonna get!'

ANSWER: _____

FILM 6

1. Although previously nominated several times, it was this film that gave Steven Spielberg his first Award as Best Director.

2. This powerful black and white film demonstrates the true horrors of war. It cleverly demonstrates the individuality of the mass victims by having one little girl in a red coat appear in the background through parts of the film.

3. The film is based on a true story of a man who managed to save around 1100 Jews from being killed at the Auschwitz concentration camp.

ANSWER: _____

FILM 7

1. This 1987 award winning film was written and produced by Oliver Stone.

2. Tom Berenger and Willem Dafoe play two sergeants from the same infantry unit with opposing ideologies of the Vietnam War.

3. This film gave, the then 20-year-old, Charlie Sheen his first big acting break.

ANSWER: _____

FILM 8

1. This film awarded its New Zealand born, Australian actor his only Academy Award to date.

2. His character quotes that he is a "husband to a murdered wife, and father to a murdered son!"

3. The film is loosely based on historical figures from the Roman Empire and takes place in AD 180.

ANSWER: _____

FILM 9

1. Along with winning Best Picture, this film also saw Clint Eastwood win Best Director, Hilary Swank win Actress in a Leading Role, and Morgan Freeman win Best Supported Actor at the 2005 ceremony.

2. Clint Eastwood was also nominated for Best Actor for his role in the film, playing a veteran Los Angeles' boxing trainer called Frankie Dunn.

3. This film caused controversy with some disability groups, as the film seemingly advocated that people with disabilities should be euthanised.

ANSWER: _____

FILM 10

1. This film was nominated in 1998 for 14 Oscars, winning 11 of them. None of the awards went to the actors involved.

2. The leading actress in the film allegedly got the part by sending the director a single rose with a card signed "From your Rose" and calling him many times saying she was the Rose he was looking for.

3. At the age of 87, Gloria Stewart became the oldest Actress to be nominated for an Oscar for her role in this film.

ANSWER: _____

FILM 11

1. This film is adapted from the sequel book to Thomas Harris' 1981 novel 'Red Dragon'.

2. It was the first "horror movie" ever to win the Best Picture Oscar.

3. It sees a young FBI trainee being helped by an imprisoned serial killer, trying to hunt down another serial killer by the name of "Buffalo Bill".

ANSWER: _____

FILM 12

1. This film saw Kathryn Bigelow win the Best Director Oscar, becoming the first female to do so.

2. The film is based on accounts from a freelance journalist who was embedded with an American bomb squad during the Iraq war for two weeks in 2004.

3. The film stars Jeremy Renner as Staff Sergeant Will James. Renner was nominated for Best Actor Oscar but lost out to Jeff Bridges for his film "Crazy Heart".

ANSWER: _____

FILM 13

1. This film saw Jessica Tandy win the Best Actress Oscar at the aged of 80 years old, at that time the oldest winner in this category.

2. It captures the relationship between a white Jewish woman and her male black chauffeur, played by Morgan Freeman, showing their unlikely friendship grow.

3. Dan Aykroyd received a nomination for Actor in a Supporting Role, for his part as Jessica Tandy's son.

    ANSWER: _____

FILM 14

1. This film was the big winner in the 1983 Oscars winning 8 of its 11 nominations.

2. This film gave Richard Attenborough his only two Oscars, one for Best Director and the other for Best Picture.

3. The film is a British-Indian historical film telling the story of the main character's struggle to win independence for India through nonviolent means.

    ANSWER: _____

FILM 15

1. This 1963 epic British historical drama won 7 Academy Awards. It is based on the true-life experiences of a British Army Officer during the First World War.

2. Peter O'Toole received a nomination for Best Actor, portraying the main character of this film.

3. Thomas Edward Lawrence, who the film is about, died in 1935 following a motorcycle accident, near his home in Dorset, England.

ANSWER: _____

FILM 16

1. This film, which is based on a true story, won 5 of its 10 Oscar nominations at the 1966 Awards.

2. The film was adapted from the book published in 1949 called "The Story of the Trapp Family".

3. The film starts in 1930s Austria, where a young novice is sent from her convent to become governess for a family of seven children.

ANSWER: _____

FILM 17

1. This film won 10 of its 11 Oscars nominations, making it the most successful musical film to date.

2. The film is loosely based on the Shakespeare romantic tragedy, "Romeo and Juliet".

3. The film tells the story of two feuding New York gangs: the "Jets" led by Riff and the "Sharks" led by Bernardo.

ANSWER: _____

FILM 18

1. This 2007 winner gave Martin Scorsese his only Oscar to date for Best Director.

2. The film has an all-star cast including: Leonardo DiCaprio, Matt Damon, Jack Nicholson, Mark Wahlberg, and Martin Sheen.

3. The film sees an undercover cop infiltrate a mob gang, run by gangster Frank Costello. At the same time Costello, played by Jack Nicholson, plants a spy within the Police Department.

ANSWER: _____

FILM 19

1. This film gave Jack Nicholson his first of three Academy Awards.

2. Louise Fletcher won the Oscar for Best Actress for her portrayal as Nurse Mildred Ratched in this film.

3. The film was mainly shot on location in Oregon State Mental Hospital, which was also the setting of the novel.

ANSWER: _____

FILM 20

1. This film was directed by Ron Howard, who won the Best Director Oscar for it in 2002.

2. Jennifer Connelly won the Oscar for Best Supporting Actress for this film.

3. Russell Crowe stars as the mathematical genius John Nash, who was diagnosed with schizophrenia.

ANSWER: _____

TRIVIA

In 2020 the film "Parasite", a black comedy thriller from South Korea, made history by becoming the first non-English speaking film to ever win the Oscar for Best Picture.

FROM THESE FILM CLUES, WHAT IS THE YEAR?

Using the three clues provided, can you work out the year?

25 to have a go at, covering the years between
1960–2020

CLUES	WHAT YEAR DID THEY TAKE PLACE?
1. Ryan O'Neil was nominated as Best Actor for "Love Story". 2. 'Woodstock', a documentary about the three-day music festival won in the category of *Best Feature Documentary*. 3. The Beatles won Best Music (Original Song Score) for 'Let It Be'.	_____
1. Robert Duvall wins the Oscar for Actor in a Leading Role for the film 'Tender Mercies'. 2. Jack Nicholson, Shirley MacLaine, and Debra Winger all starred in this year's big winner "Terms of Endearment". 3. Flashdance, wins the Oscar for Music (Original Song).	_____

1. Rocky, written by and starring Sylvester Stallone wins the Best Picture Oscar. 2. Peter Finch and Faye Dunaway both win Oscars in Leading Roles for the film "Network". 3. Robert De Niro was nominated in the category: Actor in a Leading Role for the film, Taxi Driver.	_____
1. In this year, Elizabeth Taylor won the Best Actress Oscar for the film "Who's Afraid of Virginia Woolf". 2. Actor Steve McQueen received his one and only Oscar nomination for the film "The Sandy Pebbles". 3. John Barry & Don Black win the Oscar for Music (Song) with "Born Free".	_____
1. Gary Oldman wins the Oscar for Actor in a Leading Role for the film,	

"Darkest Hour".

2. "Coco" wins the Oscar for Best Animated Feature Film.

3. "The Shape of Water" takes the Oscar for Best Picture.

———————————

1. Jodie Foster wins the award for Actress in a Leading Role, for the film "The Accused".

2. "A Fish Called Wanda" gives Kevin Kline his only Oscar to date in the category Actor in a Supporting Role.

3. Tom Hanks received his first Oscar nomination for the film "Big".

———————————

1. Sidney Poitier becomes the first black winner in the Best Actor category for his role in "Lilies of the Field".

2. Albert Finney plays the lead character in the Best Picture winning film "Tom Jones".

3. Elizabeth Taylor starred in the film, "Cleopatra"; which won 4 of the 9

———————————

awards it was nominated for.	
1. Jack Palance wins the award for Actor in a Supporting Role for his character Curly Washburn in the film "City Slickers". 2. This year saw "Silence of the Lambs" win five out of the seven awards that it was nominated for, including Best Picture, Actor in a Leading Role, and Actress in a Leading Role. 3. Geena Davis and Susan Sarandon, both received nominations for Actress in a Leading Roles for the film, "Thelma and Louise".	_____
1. Paul Newman wins Best Actor Oscar playing the character *Fast Eddie Felton*, a character who he played 25 years earlier in the film "The Hustler". 2. "Take My Breath Away" from the film Top Gun wins the Oscar for Music	_____

(Original Song).

3. "Aliens" wins two out of seven nominations, one for Sound Effects Editing, and the other for Visual Effects.

1. Michael Clarke Duncan is nominated for Actor in a Supporting Role for his character, John Coffey in the film "The Green Mile".

2. "The Matrix" wins all four of the awards that it was nominated for.

3. "Star Wars, Episode 1: The Phantom Menace", received three nominations but does not win any.

1. Warren Beatty receives two nominations for the film "Bonnie and Clyde", one for Best Actor and one for Producer.

2. Anne Bancroft and Dustin Hoffman both receive nominations for the film "The Graduate".

3. Sidney Poitier starred in two of the biggest films

of the year, "Guess Who's Coming to Dinner", and "In the Heat of the Night", but was not nominated in either.	
1. Marlon Brando wins Best Actor Oscar for his portrayal of Don Vito Corleone, in "The Godfather". 2. Bob fosse wins the Best Director Oscar for the film "Cabaret". 3. Diana Ross is nominated for the Best Actress Oscar for her portrayal as Billie Holiday in the film "Lady Sings the Blues".	_____
1. Leonardo DiCaprio is nominated in the category of Actor in a Leading Role, for his portrayal of Howard Hughes, in the film "The Aviator". 2. "Find in Netherlands" starring Johnny Depp received 7 nominations winning one, Music (Original Score). 3. Jamie Foxx is nominated	_____

in the category of Actor in a Supporting Role for the film "Collateral" and wins in the category of Actor in a Leading Role for the film "Ray" in which he plays the musician Ray Charles.

1. Robin Williams is nominated in the category of Actor in a Leading Role, for the film "Good Morning, Vietnam".
2. (I've had) The Time of My Life, from the film "Dirty Dancing" won the Oscar for Music (Original Song).
3. "The Last Emperor" won all nine of the awards that it was nominated for.

_____

1. Matthew McConaughey wins his one and only Oscar to date for the film "Dallas Buyers Club".
2. Frozen wins two Academy Awards one for Animated Feature Film and the other, for Music (Original Song) for "Let It

_____

Go". 3. "12 Years a Slave" wins the Oscar for Best Picture.	
1. Rami Malek wins, Actor in a Leading Role, for his portrayal of Freddie Mercury in the film, "Bohemian Rhapsody". 2. Olivia Colman wins her only Academy Award to date for the film "The Favourite". 3. "Green book" wins the Academy Award for Best Picture.	_____
1. Angela Bassett is nominated the category of Actress in a Leading Role, for her portrayal of Tina Turner in the film "What's Love Got to Do with It". 2. "Mrs Doubtfire" wins the Academy Award in the category of Makeup. 3. "In the Name of the Father" receives seven nominations but does not win any.	_____

1. British actor, Jim Broadbent wins his only Oscar to date, in the category of Actor in a Supporting Role for the film "Iris". 2. Shrek wins the Oscar in the category of "Animated Feature Film". 3. Will Smith is nominated in the category of Actor in a Leading Role for his portrayal of Muhammad Ali in the film "Ali".	————————
1. The film 'Avatar', directed by James Cameron wins 3 of 9 Awards in this year. 2. Sandra Bullock wins her one and only Academy Award to date for the film, "The Blind Side". 3. Jeff Bridges wins his only Oscar to date in the film "Crazy Heart". Where he played, Bad Blake, a down and out country music singer-songwriter.	————————

1. This year sees Nicolas Cage win his one and only Oscar to date, for the film "Leaving Las Vegas". 2. "Braveheart" wins 5 out of the 10 nominations that it received. 3. Kevin Spacey wins the Oscar for Actor in a Supporting Role for the film "Usual Suspects".	———————————
1. Louis Gossett Jr. wins the Oscar for Actor in a Supporting Role as, Gunnery Sergeant Emil Foley in the film "An Officer and a Gentleman". 2. "Eye of the Tiger" from "Rocky III" is nominated in the category of Music (Original Song). 3. "E.T. The Extra-Terrestrial" wins Best Director for Steven Spielberg.	———————————
1. Robert De Niro wins the	

Oscar for Actor in a Leading Role for the film "Raging Bull".

2. "Fame" wins two Academy Awards one for music (Original Song) and one for Music (Original Score).

3. Sissy Spacek receives the Oscar for Actress in a Leading Role for the film "Coal Miner's Daughter".

_____

1. West Side Story wins 10 out of the 11 Oscars that it is nomination for.

2. Audrey Hepburn is nominated for Leading Actress for the film, Breakfast at Tiffany's.

3. Judy Garland, Montgomery Clift, and Spencer Tracy all received nominations for the film, "Judgement at Nuremberg".

_____

1. This year saw Philip Seymour Hoffman win The Oscar for Actor in a Leading Role for the film "Capote".

2. "Crash" with a cast including Don Cheadle,

_____

Jennifer Esposite, Sandra Bullock and Matt Dillon, takes the Award for Best Picture.

3. Wallace and Gromit: The Curse of the Were-Rabbit, won the Oscar for Animated Feature Film.

---

1. This year's big winner was "Cabaret" winning 8 out of its 10 nominations.
2. James Caan, Robert Duvall, and Al Pacino all received nominations in the category of Actor in a Supporting Role for the film "The Godfather".
3. Both Michael Caine and Laurence Olivier were nominated in the category of Best Actor for the film "Sleuth".

_____

TRIVIA

Peter O'Toole has the most nominations of any actor for *'Actor in a Leading Role'*, with 8 nominations but has never won any.

In 2002 the Academy honoured him with an honorary award for his lifelong contribution to films.

QUESTIONS BY DECADES

Find all answers from Page 69 onwards...

1970's

1. In 1974, who at the age of 10, won the Oscar for "Actress in a Supporting Role" and is still the youngest winner of an Academy award for her role in the film *Paper Moon*?

    ....

2. In 1970, both Jon Voight and Dustin Hoffman were both nominated for the Best Actor Oscar for their roles in the same film, what was it?

    ....

3. A Clockwork Orange was nominated for four awards in 1972. Three of them were for the Best Director, Best Picture, and Writing (from another medium), all for the same person. Who was he?

    ....

4. 1973 saw Diana Ross nominated for her portrayal of Billie Holiday in which film?

    ....

5. In 1972 the winner of Music (Song, Original for the Picture) was won for the theme from the film 'Shaft'. Who won it?

    ....

6. In which year was 'The Exorcist' nominated for 10 Oscars, winning two of them?

   ....

7. Ingrid Bergman won the Oscar for *Actress in a Supporting Role* in 1975, for which Agatha Christie film starring Albert Finney as the main character?

   ....

8. Which British actress won 2 Best Actress Academy Awards in the 1970s for the films "Woman in Love" (1971, and "A Touch of Class" (1974)?

   ....

9. For the 1978 Oscars, who won the Academy Award for best director for the film Annie Hall?

   ....

10. Who was nominated in in 1979 in the category of *Actor in a Leading Role* for his portrayal of Buddy Holly in the film "The Buddy Holly Story"?

   ....

1980's

1. Who starred in, and was nominated for, Best Actor playing John Merrick in the film "Elephant Man"?

    ....

2. 1982 saw Henry Fonda and Katharine Hepburn both win leading role Oscars for which film?

    ....

3. In 1980 Bette Midler was nominated for *Actress in a Leading role* for the film 'The Rose'. The film was loosely based on the life of which late 1960s rock star?

    ....

4. In 1981 Robert Redford won his only Academy Award for directing which film?

    ....

5. Steven Spielberg, Kathleen Kennedy, Frank Marshall, and Quincy Jones produced which film that in 1986 was nominated for 11 Oscars but did not win any?

    ....

6. In 1982, John Gielgud won the Academy Award for Actor in a Supporting Role for the film Arthur. Which British Actor played the Leading Role?

    ....

7. Which singer-songwriter won the Academy Award for original song in 1986 for their song, "Say You, Say Me"?

    ....

8. In 1985 Haing S. Ngor won the Oscar for *Actor in a Supporting Role* for playing the real-life character Dith Pran in which film?

    ....

9. 1986 sees Oprah Winfrey in her acting debut receive a nomination for Actress in a Supporting Role, for which Steven Spielberg film?

    ....

10. Michael Douglas wins the Oscar for Actor in a Leading Role in 1988 playing Gordon Gekko in which film?

    ....

1990's

1. In 1990 Daniel Day Lewis won his first of three Academy Awards for *Actor in a Leading Role* for which film?

   ....

2. In 1993 the winner of Music Original Song was won by "A Whole New World" from which film?

   ....

3. "When We Were Kings" won the Academy Award for Documentary (Feature). The film is a boxing documentary about the 1974 world heavyweight championship bout between which two boxers?

   ....

4. In 1999 Steven Spielberg won best director for the film "Saving Private Ryan". Which actor played the title role?

   ....

5. "Show me the money" is a famous line from which film that starred Tom Cruise and Cuba Gooding, JR, in which Gooding won the Academy Award for Actor in a Supporting Role?

   ....

6. Jon Bon Jovi was nominated for Music (Original Song) for the song "Blaze of Glory" from which movie?

    ....

7. Kathy Bates won the Best Actress Oscar for which Horror/Thriller film, that starred James Caan as a novelist who after a car crash, Bates, a former nurse, rescues and claims to be his biggest fan, but things turn dark when she finds he's going to kill off her favourite character from his novels.

    ....

8. In 1991 Whoopi Goldberg won the Oscar in the category of *Actress in a Supporting Role* for the film "Ghost". What was the name of her character?

    ....

9. Who was nominated for Best Actor Oscar in 1993 for his portrayal of Malcolm X in the film of the same name?

    ....

10. Which film at the 1991 Academy Awards was Kevin Costner nominated in the categories of Best Actor but did not win, and Best Director which he did?

    ....

2000's

1. Ken Watanabe was nominated for *Actor in a Supporting Role*, as the character Katsumoto in which 2004 Tom Cruise film?

   ....

2. Joaquin Phoenix and Reese Witherspoon, for which she won the 2006 Best Actress Oscar, starred in a biographical film about which singer?

   ....

3. Heath Ledger tragically died before winning Actor in a Supporting Role as which character in the film 'The Dark Knight'?

   ....

4. Which film saw Julia Roberts win her only Oscar to date in 2001?

   ....

5. In 2001, Bob Dylan won the Oscar for music (original song) for the song 'Things Have Changed' from which Michael Douglas movie?

   ....

6. Crouching Tiger, Hidden Dragon won best foreign language film in which year?

   ....

7. In 2003, which film won Animated Feature Film, beating the likes of 'Lilo and Stitch' and 'Ice Age'? It's the first non-English language and hand-drawn film to win the award.

   ....

8. Peter Jackson won best director for the big winner of 2004; the film won all 11 Oscars it was nominated for. What was the film?

   ....

9. Adrien Brody won the best actor Oscar in 2003 for which film?

   ....

10. Heath Ledger and Jake Gyllenhaal starred in which film that saw Ang Lee win the Best Director Oscar at the 2006 Academy Awards?

    ....

2010's

1. Invictus starring Morgan Freeman and Matt Damon was set around which sporting event.

    ....

2. In 2010 there were 10 nominations for Best Picture, but what was the only animated film to be nominated for it?

    ....

3. 2013 saw the film "Lincoln" received 12 nominations, one of which was for actor in a leading role. Who played Lincoln?

    ....

4. Randy Newman receives the Oscar for music (original song) for 'We Belong Together' from which animated Movie?

    ....

5. Meryl Streep wins actress in a leading role in 2012 for portraying which historical figure?

    ....

6. Matthew McConaughey, in 2014, won the Best Actor Oscar for which film?

   ....

7. What was the name of the real-life character that Leonardo DiCaprio portrayed in the film 'The Wolf of Wall Street'?

   ....

8. Chiwetel Ejiofor was nominated in 2014 for *Actor in a Leading Role* for his performance in the film which won Best Picture Oscar, what was the film?

   ....

9. The theory of everything saw Eddie Redmayne win Best Actor in a leading role for the portrayal of which famous scientist?

   ....

10. Frances McDormand won her second of three Oscars for Actress in a Leading Role for which film in 2018?

    ....

WORDSEARCHES

Best supporting Actor Winners

Try finding these following Best Supporting Actors' surnames in the Wordsearch below...

F	G	S	A	C	W	I	L	L	I	A	M	S	K	Y
R	D	L	V	X	A	W	D	L	B	M	U	T	O	S
V	F	E	N	U	H	I	Y	H	L	S	W	R	D	T
T	P	H	M	I	B	A	T	O	I	S	V	Q	E	K
F	E	N	W	V	C	O	N	N	E	R	Y	M	N	E
G	S	H	N	W	M	H	R	C	A	T	W	J	I	N
H	C	T	F	E	B	D	O	C	H	K	R	D	R	I
E	I	N	D	T	F	H	H	L	D	O	Y	S	O	A
S	D	R	G	K	L	G	A	R	S	D	V	K	J	C
D	A	M	A	J	N	Y	H	K	V	O	H	B	Y	N
B	G	I	E	L	G	U	D	H	F	L	N	O	N	I
Y	R	L	N	M	B	R	C	T	Y	B	V	S	Y	L
O	D	L	T	S	J	O	D	L	B	H	T	X	R	K
T	K	S	C	A	O	G	H	T	K	L	I	N	E	H
R	M	I	L	B	T	K	S	J	R	N	G	D	Y	H

1. Jack NICHOLSON 1984
2. Sean CONNERY 1988
3. Robert DE NIRO 1975
4. John GIELGUD 1982
5. John MILLS 1971

6. Kevin KLINE 1989
7. Joe PESCI 1991
8. Robin WILLIAMS 1998
9. Michael CAINE 1987
10. Javier BARDEM 2008

Best Supporting Actress Winners

Try finding these following Best Supporting Actress Winners' surnames in the wordsearch below...

K	M	F	C	C	K	M	D	H	L	C	K	T	I	G
W	A	E	B	O	U	A	T	H	U	D	F	K	S	U
H	U	H	S	D	L	O	G	B	Y	D	K	H	L	N
A	D	K	S	T	R	E	E	P	D	H	S	A	W	I
S	F	U	I	H	T	H	M	F	C	N	W	O	T	E
Y	D	M	K	U	E	Q	W	A	R	E	B	X	N	R
A	L	O	T	A	F	N	U	K	N	I	L	I	H	R
W	L	A	G	S	K	A	L	N	K	L	A	G	N	E
A	H	L	N	K	D	I	M	E	Q	O	W	U	S	G
H	B	I	X	G	I	H	S	U	C	J	M	R	H	N
T	K	W	M	W	E	N	B	M	T	T	R	C	O	I
A	O	L	T	D	A	V	I	S	K	S	N	K	M	S
H	T	K	G	J	V	K	R	F	J	E	B	U	N	A
C	W	N	D	R	A	K	O	B	D	K	Q	F	M	B
K	V	C	H	T	C	G	D	T	F	S	R	O	S	G

1. Olivia COLEMAN 2019
2. Olympia DUKAKIS 1988
3. Judi DENCH 1999
4. Angelina JOLIE 2000
5. Jessica LANGE 1983
6. Meryl STREEP 1980
7. Geena DAVIS 1989
8. Kim BASINGER 1998
9. Jennifer HUDSON 2007
10. Anne HATHAWAY 2013

Winners of Animated Feature Film

Try finding these following winners of Animated Feature Films in the Wordsearch below...

A	E	C	H	A	P	P	Y	F	E	E	T	L	I	Q
R	G	X	D	E	R	E	W	I	H	E	R	A	P	T
Y	S	D	G	E	H	A	F	R	A	U	G	K	E	H
W	G	F	I	N	D	I	N	G	N	E	M	O	H	E
T	B	H	I	U	E	T	E	G	F	S	H	E	J	I
H	H	B	E	Y	C	T	G	A	O	A	J	N	W	N
N	W	T	R	A	T	A	T	O	U	I	L	L	E	C
E	C	P	Y	A	A	P	V	R	J	P	W	V	U	R
D	U	O	E	C	V	L	H	F	E	O	J	C	E	E
N	E	T	C	H	U	E	E	A	R	T	M	G	B	D
E	O	Z	C	O	W	I	K	F	E	O	I	P	M	I
E	P	Y	S	H	T	E	J	R	Q	O	Z	R	L	B
R	Y	C	A	D	R	Y	Z	U	G	Z	B	E	D	L
G	E	U	Y	H	E	Y	V	K	J	R	N	I	N	E
S	B	N	S	P	D	N	E	E	T	J	W	A	G	S

1. SHREK (2002)
2. RATATOUILLE (2008)
3. BRAVE (2013)
4. ZOOTOPIA (2017)
5. RANGO (2012)
6. THE INCREDIBLES (2005)
7. FROZEN (2014)
8. FINDING NEMO (2004)
9. COCO (2018)
10. HAPPY FEET (2007)

Directors Who Have Won the Most Oscars

Try find the surnames of the following 10 director winners...

E	N	M	D	W	E	N	G	C	N	N	F	B	N	E
E	D	R	P	D	A	U	S	W	I	L	D	E	R	L
O	O	S	C	O	P	P	O	L	A	B	L	S	H	L
F	I	R	E	A	A	E	H	S	W	S	M	E	D	O
E	C	K	P	N	P	R	R	T	G	F	U	E	E	Y
D	A	G	J	R	F	R	L	O	C	B	Y	G	A	H
B	M	O	T	A	H	E	A	R	Y	W	G	W	S	E
G	E	L	K	F	S	O	T	E	H	R	J	N	T	G
E	R	V	H	N	R	E	J	P	E	N	B	O	W	O
B	O	X	T	H	F	G	T	B	G	W	S	S	O	R
M	N	E	S	E	O	N	L	G	E	F	V	K	O	E
Y	M	L	W	Y	L	E	R	W	I	N	E	C	D	U
D	S	O	W	H	I	E	L	W	O	F	A	A	F	G
S	F	C	R	P	I	L	F	J	U	J	K	J	I	A
G	L	Y	S	D	E	A	N	K	D	T	A	F	K	O

1. James CAMERON
2. Steven SPIELBERG
3. William WYLER
4. Peter JACKSON
5. Ang LEE

6. Clint EASTWOOD
7. Francis Ford COPPOLA
8. Billy WILDER
9. John FORD
10. Frank CAPRA

Animated Films that won the Oscar for Best Song

Find these Animated films (only the words in CAPITAL LETTERS) that have won the Oscar for Music (Song), or Music (Original Song) - the category name has changed through the years.

N	D	A	J	N	N	O	Z	R	A	T	N	H	F	H
R	S	F	O	T	L	A	N	D	S	R	N	C	A	I
J	G	H	R	F	S	J	I	A	U	G	N	C	B	A
N	M	S	R	O	D	N	E	L	E	R	I	G	P	N
L	E	P	N	H	Z	B	F	S	Z	R	N	U	B	I
G	J	U	I	H	G	E	M	K	F	I	S	Y	G	S
W	G	H	D	N	N	G	N	A	K	D	D	E	A	N
A	V	N	D	A	O	T	H	H	J	I	X	T	I	E
L	F	A	A	D	G	C	U	T	A	G	N	N	F	G
E	H	Z	L	F	U	R	C	M	I	O	O	A	T	R
S	J	R	A	O	H	W	R	I	H	C	O	Z	P	A
V	S	A	S	U	S	E	D	A	O	A	R	F	Y	B
E	F	T	U	Y	M	H	C	C	D	R	P	A	G	V
Y	B	H	A	T	S	O	S	J	A	G	L	A	E	H
I	D	N	A	L	P	E	Z	W	E	N	D	D	J	O

1. PINOCCIO (1941)
2. The Little MERMAID (1990)
3. Beauty and the BEAST (1992)
4. ALADDIN (1993)
5. The Lion KING (1995)
6. POCAHONTAS (1996)
7. The Prince of EGYPT (1999)
8. TARZAN (2000)
9. FROZEN (2014)
10. COCO (2018)

Best of British (ACTRESSES)

Below are 10 British Oscar winning actresses, can you find their surnames in the grid below?

R	W	B	B	E	W	W	I	N	S	L	E	T	M	T
I	F	N	J	B	M	S	A	F	D	G	L	O	O	E
C	J	E	E	S	F	E	M	H	H	G	G	A	O	T
H	O	T	N	L	W	R	S	I	K	J	N	M	R	J
A	E	L	D	R	L	U	O	T	T	O	F	M	E	N
R	B	H	M	J	V	U	N	H	S	H	B	Y	B	H
D	M	W	D	A	A	L	C	K	W	E	N	N	H	A
S	F	R	T	T	N	N	C	T	F	R	S	E	T	V
O	E	S	N	I	H	A	G	K	H	K	G	R	R	I
N	B	D	Y	H	J	O	J	Y	A	R	B	R	O	L
W	B	V	G	W	J	W	M	E	J	N	M	I	W	L
A	E	I	L	G	U	R	E	P	E	G	T	M	S	A
L	E	T	A	N	D	Y	G	S	S	E	G	Y	N	N
L	H	R	W	R	R	L	J	N	G	O	S	O	U	D
H	N	M	D	O	E	L	C	A	M	O	N	L	F	J

1. Maggie SMITH
2. Glenda JACKSON
3. Jessica TANDY
4. Emma THOMPSON
5. Helen MIRREN

6. Kate WINSLET
7. Julianne MOORE
8. Olivia COLMAN
9. Olivia de HAVILLAND
10. Vivien LEIGH

Best of British (ACTORS)

Below are 10 British Oscar winning actors, can you find their surnames in the grid below?

R	E	B	D	O	N	M	W	F	I	R	T	H	A	I
W	T	Y	I	G	G	M	A	H	G	R	I	B	G	K
F	Y	S	E	K	O	U	P	D	T	E	O	D	R	H
S	N	N	G	G	I	H	I	G	R	C	H	N	H	A
H	H	I	W	L	W	S	F	N	W	E	J	T	S	R
R	S	K	R	P	F	R	I	J	N	L	K	K	T	R
E	F	P	I	J	M	P	N	G	T	E	O	D	G	I
D	V	O	E	N	R	U	C	E	P	N	S	H	E	S
M	U	H	B	G	G	O	H	S	T	F	R	S	E	O
A	Y	B	H	W	J	S	W	T	N	K	D	D	H	N
Y	B	D	K	P	G	H	L	A	B	U	H	N	S	R
N	L	I	U	T	R	T	M	E	J	T	D	R	J	H
E	E	U	R	R	D	D	D	A	Y	L	E	W	I	S
S	S	T	B	Y	L	S	M	A	I	L	L	I	W	E
O	A	Y	K	O	V	J	L	O	L	E	J	L	K	S

1. Ben KINGSLEY	6. Eddie REDMAYNE
2. Daniel DAY LEWIS	7. Gary OLDMAN
3. Jeremy IRONS	8. Peter FINCH
4. Anthony HOPKINS	9. Rex HARRISON
5. Colin FIRTH	10. Alec GUINNESS

Actors Who Have Never Won an Acting Oscar

Can you find the surnames of the 10 actors listed below that have never won an Acting Oscar. Some have received Oscars in other categories but not for their Acting skills.

G	E	H	S	J	U	N	K	H	J	E	R	K	I	J
R	Y	D	R	D	O	A	L	S	T	N	A	R	G	E
T	L	J	K	S	P	T	J	C	R	U	I	S	E	T
W	K	M	E	K	I	H	D	H	H	R	C	H	T	G
B	J	E	Y	D	R	J	F	D	E	T	V	C	E	H
G	N	R	R	H	E	K	K	D	E	E	T	E	I	S
S	E	Y	I	N	N	G	N	R	K	P	P	R	Y	J
T	T	K	Y	O	L	E	W	H	K	J	P	T	T	A
E	Y	F	T	O	B	Y	R	F	A	S	K	H	A	C
H	L	R	H	S	H	N	Y	E	E	H	S	E	T	K
L	O	D	S	L	O	Y	B	U	R	E	D	K	R	S
N	Y	A	R	M	Y	E	H	J	B	R	Y	E	U	O
D	F	H	A	R	R	E	L	S	O	N	A	G	O	N
B	E	D	U	E	D	K	O	F	I	E	S	P	C	J
J	I	H	J	N	E	F	L	J	T	H	I	E	H	O

1.	Edward NORTON	6.	Tom CRUISE
2.	Woody HARRELSON	7.	Samual L JACKSON
3.	Michael FASSBENDER	8.	Matt DAMON
4.	Stanley TUCCI	9.	Johnny DEPP
5.	Liam NEESON	10.	Harrison FORD

Actresses Who Have Never Won an Acting Oscar

Can you find the surnames of the 10 actresses listed below that have never won an acting Oscar!

Y	H	J	T	W	I	C	K	E	N	H	A	M	N	J
E	M	O	R	D	M	I	D	L	E	R	A	T	S	D
C	U	B	J	B	H	P	R	T	S	A	G	J	O	S
N	M	C	R	R	A	Y	F	I	E	L	D	M	J	O
A	U	O	L	G	B	N	M	E	V	E	R	A	P	N
W	I	L	H	O	M	I	L	L	I	N	I	U	M	O
E	D	L	H	C	S	U	I	L	H	F	B	F	R	S
A	A	E	G	T	H	E	S	D	G	T	A	R	W	S
V	T	T	O	H	T	M	E	D	N	G	E	A	G	N
E	S	T	E	L	A	I	S	P	A	F	T	I	U	A
R	B	E	L	I	N	N	E	Y	F	T	L	O	D	H
A	N	W	L	O	T	P	W	I	S	Y	S	P	I	O
T	F	L	T	C	H	N	E	K	I	Y	G	Z	D	J
S	I	E	H	Y	I	F	N	E	R	S	L	O	N	D
W	C	I	P	M	P	L	O	O	I	D	A	T	S	A

1. Michelle WILLIAMS
2. Laura LINNEY
3. Amy ADAMS
4. Naomi WATTS
5. Toni COLLETTE

6. Glenn CLOSE
7. Michelle PFEIFFER
8. Scarlett JOHANSSON
9. Sigourney WEAVER
10. Bette MIDLER

Winners From the Golden Age of the Cinema

Can you find the surnames of the Actors and Actresses that won best acting Oscars during the golden age of the cinema, between 1935 to 1955.

Y	H	Y	B	R	A	C	R	A	W	F	O	R	D	G
Y	N	G	R	M	A	E	B	E	C	D	A	L	A	B
E	R	S	D	F	N	M	K	I	U	D	A	R	T	U
S	B	G	U	I	M	H	G	R	D	G	T	V	S	O
R	L	N	A	Y	G	F	T	Y	H	G	C	R	I	H
O	D	I	R	B	I	B	J	G	N	A	R	O	P	S
H	O	R	I	Z	L	N	I	A	L	N	O	R	R	F
L	W	L	T	N	B	E	O	O	L	R	S	L	Y	N
E	C	L	R	R	L	T	A	E	B	U	B	L	I	A
M	O	I	A	O	S	J	L	S	U	B	Y	O	T	M
M	O	T	C	B	X	L	G	U	E	P	R	D	E	G
O	P	S	Y	A	A	F	W	H	A	E	T	G	B	R
P	E	Y	J	R	T	O	R	M	I	H	O	S	J	E
R	R	A	A	S	J	L	P	R	K	H	K	B	H	B
O	P	P	S	R	S	T	E	W	A	R	T	U	M	M

1. Clark GABLE
2. Bette DAVIS
3. Spencer TRACY
4. Vivien LEIGH
5. Bing CROSBY

6. James STEWART
7. Ingrid BERGMAN
8. Gary COOPER
9. Joan CRAWFORD
5. Audrey HEPBURN

ANSWERS

BEST PICTURE WINNERS

1. Kramer v Kramer
2. Ben Hur
3. Patton
4. Godfather part 2
5. Forrest Gump
6. Schindler's List
7. Platoon
8. Gladiator
9. Million Dollar Baby
10. Titanic
11. Silence of the Lambs
12. The Hurt Locker
13. Driving Miss Daisy
14. Gandhi
15. Lawrance of Arabia
16. The Sound of Music
17. West Side Story
18. The Departed
19. One Flew Over the Cuckoo's Nest
20. A Beautiful Mind

FROM THESE FILM CLUES, WHAT IS THE YEAR?

CLUES	WHAT YEAR DID THEY TAKE PLACE?
1. Ryan O'Neil was nominated as Best Actor for "Love Story". 2. 'Woodstock', a documentary about the three-day music festival won in the category of Best Feature Documentary. 3. The Beatles won Best Music (Original Song Score) for 'Let It Be'.	**1971**
1. Robert Duvall wins the Oscar for - Actor in a Leading Role for the film 'Tender Mercies'. 2. Jack Nicholson, Shirley MacLaine, and Debra Winger all starred in this year's big winner "Terms of Endearment". 3. Flashdance, wins the Oscar for Music (Original Song).	**1984**
1. Rocky, written by and starring Sylvester Stallone	

wins the Best Picture Oscar. 2. Peter Finch and Faye Dunaway both win Oscars in Leading Roles for the film "Network". 3. Robert De Niro was nominated in the category, Actor in a Leading Role for the film, Taxi Driver.	**1977**
1. In this year Elizabeth Taylor won the Best Actress Oscar for the film "Who's Afraid of Virginia Woolf". 2. Actor, Steve McQueen received his one and only Oscar nomination for the film "The Sandy Pebbles". 3. John Barry & Don Black win the Oscar for Music (Song) with "Born Free".	**1967**
1. Gary Oldman wins the Oscar for Actor in a Leading Role for the film, "Darkest Hour". 2. "Coco" wins the Oscar for Best Animated Feature Film. 3. "The Shape of Water" takes the Oscar for Best	**2018**

Picture.	
1. Jodie Foster wins the award for Actress in a Leading Role, for the film "The Accused". 2. "A Fish Called Wanda" gives Kevin Kline his only Oscar to date. in the category Actor in a Supporting Role. 3. Tom Hanks received his first Oscar nomination for the film "Big".	**1989**
1. Sidney Poitier becomes the first black winner in the Best Actor category for his role in "Lilies of the Field". 2. Albert Finney plays the lead character in the Best Picture winning film "Tom Jones". 3. Elizabeth Taylor starred in the film, "Cleopatra". Which won four of the nine awards it was nominated for.	**1964**
1. Jack Palance wins the award for Actor in a	

Supporting Role for his character Curly Washburn in the film "City Slickers". 2. This year saw "Silence of the Lambs" win five out of the seven awards that it was nominated for, including Best Picture, Actor in a Leading Role, and Actress in a Leading Role. 3. Geena Davis and Susan Sarandon, both received nominations for Actress in a Leading Roles for the film, "Thelma and Louise".	**1992**
1. Paul Newman wins Best Actor Oscar playing the character, Fast Eddie Felton, a character who he played 25 years earlier in the film "The Hustler". 2. "Take My Breath Away" from the film Top Gun wins the Oscar for Music (Original Song). 3. "Aliens" wins two out of seven nominations, one for Sound Effects Editing, and the other for Visual	**1987**

Effects.	
1. Michael Clarke Duncan is nominated for, Actor in a Supporting Role for his character, John Coffey in the film "The Green Mile". 2. "The Matrix" wins all four of the awards that it was nominated for. 3. "Star Wars, Episode 1: The Phantom Menace", received three nominations but does not win any.	**2000**
1. Warren Beatty receives two nominations for the film "Bonnie and Clyde", one for Best Actor and one for Producer. 2. Anne Bancroft and Dustin Hoffman both receive nominations for the film "The Graduate". 3. Sidney Poitier starred in two of the biggest films of the year, "Guess Who's Coming to Dinner", and "In the Heat of the Night", but was not	**1968**

nominated in either.	
1. Marlon Brando wins Best Actor Oscar for his portrayal of Don Vito Corleone, in "The Godfather". 2. Bob fosse wins the best director Oscar for the film "Cabaret". 3. Diana Ross is nominated for the Best Actress Oscar for her portrayal as Billie Holiday in the film "Lady Sings the Blues".	**1973**
1. Leonardo DiCaprio is nominated in the category of Actor in a Leading Role, for his portrayal of Howard Hughes, in the film "The Aviator". 2. "Find in Netherlands" starring Johnny Depp received 7 nominations winning one, Music (Original Score). 3. Jamie Foxx is nominated in the category of Actor in a Supporting Role for the film "Collateral" and wins in the category of	**2005**

Actor in a Leading Role for the film "Ray" in which he plays the musician Ray Charles.	
1. Robin Williams is nominated in the category of, Actor in a Leading Role, for the film "Good Morning, Vietnam". 2. (I've had) The Time of My Life, from the film "Dirty Dancing" won the Oscar for Music (Original Song). 3. "The Last Emperor" won all nine of the awards that it was nominated for.	**1988**
1. Matthew McConaughey wins his one and only Oscar to date for the film "Dallas Buyers Club". 2. Frozen wins two Academy Awards one for, Animated Feature Film and the other, for Music (Original Song) for "Let It Go". 3. "12 Years a Slave" wins the Oscar for Best	**2014**

Picture.	
1. Rami Malek wins, Actor in a Leading Role, for his portrayal of Freddie Mercury in the film, "Bohemian Rhapsody". 2. Olivia Colman wins her only Academy Award to date for the film "The Favourite". 3. "Green book" wins the Academy Award for Best Picture.	**2019**
1. Angela Bassett is nominated the category of Actress in a Leading Role, for her portrayal of Tina Turner in the film "What's Love Got to Do with It". 2. "Mrs Doubtfire" wins the Academy Award in the category of, Makeup. 3. "In the Name of the Father" receives seven nominations but does not win any.	**1994**
1. British actor, Jim Broadbent wins his only	

Oscar to date, In the category of, Actor in a Supporting Role for the film "Iris". 2. Shrek wins the Oscar in the category of "Animated Feature Film". 3. Will Smith is nominated in the category of Actor in a Leading Role for his portrayal of Muhammad Ali in the film "Ali".	**2002**
1. The film, 'Avatar', directed by James Cameron wins 3 of 9 Awards in this year. 2. Sandra Bullock wins her one and only Academy Award to date for the film, "The blind side". 3. Jeff Bridges wins his only Oscar to date in the film "Crazy Heart". Where he played, Bad Blake, a down and out country music singer-songwriter.	**2010**
1. This year sees Nicolas Cage win his one and only Oscar to date, for the film" Leaving Las Vegas". 2. "Braveheart" wins 5 out	

of the 10 nominations that it received. 3. Kevin Spacey wins the Oscar for Actor in a Supporting Role for the film "Usual Suspects".	**1996**
1. Louis Gossett Jr. wins the Oscar for Actor in a Supporting Role as, Gunnery Sergeant Emil Foley in the film "An Officer and a Gentleman". 2. "Eye of the Tiger" from "Rocky III" is nominated in the category of, Music (Original Song). 3. "E.T. The Extra-Terrestrial" wins Best Director for Steven Spielburg.	**1983**
1. Robert De Niro wins the Oscar for Actor in a Leading Role for the film "Raging Bull". 2. "Fame" wins 2 Academy Awards one for Music (Original Song) and one for Music (Original Score). 3. Sissy Spacek receives the	**1981**

Oscar for, Actress in a Leading Role for the film "Coal Miner's Daughter".	
1. West Side Story wins 10 out of the 11 Oscars that it is nomination for. 2. Audrey Hepburn is nominated for Leading Actress for the film, Breakfast at Tiffany's. 3. Judy Garland, Montgomery Clift, and Spencer Tracy all received nominations for the film, "Judgement at Nuremberg".	**1962**
1. This year saw Philip Seymour Hoffman win The Oscar for Actor in a Leading Role for the film "Capote". 2. "Crash" with a cast including, Don Cheadle, Jennifer Esposite, Sandra Bullock, and Matt Dillon, takes the Award for Best Picture. 3. Wallace and Gromit: The Curse of the Were-Rabbit, won the Oscar for	**2006**

Animated Feature Film.	
1. This year's big winner was "Cabaret" winning 8 out of its 10 nominations. 2. James Caan, Robert Duvall, and Al Pacino all received nominations in the category of Actor in a Supporting Role for the film "The Godfather". 3. Both Michael Caine and Laurence Olivier were nominated in the category of Best Actor for the film "Sleuth".	**1973**

QUESTIONS BY DECADES

ANSWERS

1970's

1. Tatum O'Neal

2. Midnight cowboy

3. Stanley Kubrick

4. Lady sings the Blues.

5. Isaac Hayes

6. 1974

7. Murder on the Orient express

8. Glenda Jackson

9. Woody Allen

10. Gary Busey

1980's

1. John Hurt

2. On Golden Pond

3. Janis Joplin

4. Ordinary People

5. The Colour Purple

6. Dudley Moore

7. Lionel Richie

8. The Killing Fields

9. The Colour Purple

10. Wall Street

1990's

1. My Left Foot

2. Aladdin

3. George Foreman & Muhammad Ali

4. Matt Damon

5. Jerry Maguire

6. Young guns II

7. Misery

8. Oda Mae Brown

9. Denzel Washington

10. Dances with Wolves

2000's

1. The Last Samurai

2. Johnny Cash

3. The Joker

4. Erin Brockovich

5. Wonder Boys

6. 2001

7. Spirited Away

8. Lord of the Rings Return of the King

9. The Pianist

10. Brokeback Mountain

2010's

1. 1995 Rugby Union World Cup

2. Up

3. Daniel Day-Lewis

4. Toy Story 3

5. Margaret Thatcher

6. Dallas Buyers Club

7. Jordan Belfort

8. 12 Years a Slave

9. Steven Hawkins

10. Three Billboards Outside Ebbing, Missouri.

WORDSEARCH

ANSWERS

Best supporting Actor Winners

PAGE 43.

				W	I	L	L	I	A	M	S		
		N								D			
	P		I							E			
	E			C	O	N	N	E	R	Y	N	E	
	S			M	H					I	N		
	C		E		O					R	I		
	I		D			L				O	A		
		R					S				C		
	A	M					O						
B	G	I	E	L	G	U	D			N			
		L											
		L											
		S				K	L	I	N	E			

Best Supporting Actress Winners

PAGE 44.

		C				H						
			O				U					
				L				D				
	D	S	T	R	E	E	P		S			
		U				M				O		
Y		K				A	E				N	
A	L		A				N	I				R
W	A				K				L			E
A		N				I			O			G
H			G			S			J		H	N
T				E						C		I
A			D	A	V	I	S		N			S
H								E				A
							D					B

Winners of Animated Feature Film

PAGE 45.

			H	A	P	P	Y	F	E	E	T	
						R						T
						A						H
	F	I	N	D	I	N	G	N	E	M	O	E
						G						I
	B					O		A				N
	R	A	T	A	T	O	U	I	L	L	E	C
C	A							P				R
O	V							O		F		E
C	E							T		R		D
O		K						O		O		I
		E						O		Z		B
		R						Z		E		L
		H								N		E
		S										S

Directors Who Have Won the Most Oscars

PAGE 46.

		D										
	R						W	I	L	D	E	R
	O	C	O	P	P	O	L	A		L		
F			A								E	
	C			P								E
	A				R							A
	M					A				G		S
	E								R		N	T
	R							E			O	W
	O						B				S	O
	N					L					K	O
		W	Y	L	E	R					C	D
				I							A	
			P								J	
		S										

Animated Films that won the Oscar for Best Song

PAGE 47.

										T			
		F							S				
			R					A					
				O			E					G	
		P	N		Z	B					N		
			I			E				I			S
			D	N			N		K		D		A
		N	D		O					I		T	
		A	A			C		A			N		
		Z	L				C	M		O	O		T
		R	A				R	I	H	C			P
		A				E		A	O				Y
		T			M		C	C					G
						O							E
					P								

Best of British (ACTRESSES)

PAGE 48.

					W	I	N	S	L	E	T	M	
						S						O	
C						M						O	
	O					I					N	R	
		L				T	O					E	
		M				S	H						H
			A				K				N		A
			T	N		C					E		V
			H	A							R		I
			H	J	O						R		L
			G				M				I		L
		I				P					M		A
	E	T	A	N	D	Y			S				N
L										O			D
										N			

Best of British (ACTORS)

PAGE 49.

						F	I	R	T	H
			G					R		
	S			U				O		H
	N				I				N	A
	I				F	N			S	R
R	K				I		N			R
E	P	I			N		E			I
D	O		N		C			S		S
M	H		G		H				S	O
A				S		N				N
Y					L	A				
N					M	E				
E		D	D	A	Y	L	E	W	I	S
			L							
			O							

Actors Who Have Never Won an Acting Oscar

PAGE 50.

					N							
				O				T				
			S				C	R	U	I	S	E
		E							R	C		
	E						D	E			C	
	N						D	E			I	
				N		N			P			J
			O		E				P			A
		T		B								C
		R	S		N							K
	O		S	O					D			S
N		A	M						R			O
	F	H	A	R	R	E	L	S	O	N		N
		D					F					

Actresses Who Have Never Won an Acting Oscar

PAGE 51.

				M	I	D	L	E	R			
									A			
		C								D		
		O	L							A		N
W		L		O							M	O
E		L		S								S
A		E			E	S				R	W	S
V		T			M					E	A	N
E		T		A				F	T			A
R		E	L	I	N	N	E	Y	F	T		H
			L			I	S					O
		L			E							J
	I				F							
W				P								

Winners From the Golden Age of the Cinema

PAGE 52.

				C	R	A	W	F	O	R	D
								D			
									A		
	G									V	
		A					H		C		I
			B			G			R		S
				L	I			N	O		
		T		E				R	S		N
C		R	L					U	B		A
O		A						B	Y		M
O		C						P			G
P		Y						E			R
E								H			E
R											B
				S	T	E	W	A	R	T	

Printed in Great Britain
by Amazon

39271939R00050